GREAT WHITE SHARKS

ELIZABETH THOMAS

Published in the United States of America by Cherry Lake Publishing
Ann Arbor, Michigan
www.cherrylakepublishing.com

Consultants: Dominique A. Didier, PhD, Associate Professor, Department of Biology, Millersville University; Marla Conn, ReadAbility, Inc.
Editorial direction: Red Line Editorial
Book design and illustration: Sleeping Bear Press

Photo Credits: Todd Winner/iStockphoto, cover, 1, 14; iStockphoto/Thinkstock, 5, 11, 24, 27; Sleeping Bear Press, 7; Shutterstock Images, 9; Dorling Kindersley RF/Thinkstock, 13; Peter Nile/iStockphoto, 17; Dan Callister/Rex Features/AP Images, 19; Jim Agronick/Shutterstock Images, 21; Fuse/Thinkstock, 23; Design Pics/Thinkstock, 25; Emmanuel R. Lacoste/Shutterstock Images, 28; iStockphoto, 29

Library of Congress Cataloging-in-Publication Data
Thomas, Elizabeth.
  Great white sharks / Elizabeth Thomas.
      p. cm. — (Exploring our oceans)
Audience: 009.
Audience: Grades 4 to 6.
Includes index.
ISBN 978-1-62431-407-0 (hardcover) — ISBN 978-1-62431-483-4 (pbk.) — ISBN 978-1-62431-445-2 (pdf) — ISBN 978-1-62431-521-3 (ebook)
1. White shark—Juvenile literature. I. Title.

QL638.95.L3T475 2014
597.3'3—dc23   2013008486

Cherry Lake Publishing would like to acknowledge the work of
The Partnership for 21st Century Skills. Please visit www.p21.org
for more information.

Printed in the United States of America
Corporate Graphics Inc.
July 2013
CLFA11

ABOUT THE AUTHOR

Elizabeth Thomas is the author of several books for children. She received her master of fine arts in Writing for Children and Young Adults from Hamline University. Currently, she lives on Cape Cod in Massachusetts.

TABLE OF CONTENTS

CHAPTER 1

A Fierce Creature

Early one August morning, a surfer sat on his board with his legs dangling over the sides. He was scanning the California horizon for the next set of waves. Suddenly, he noticed his board had stopped bobbing in the current. He looked down. To his horror, he saw a great white shark biting his board. Its head was almost 3 feet (0.9 m) across.

The shark had surfaced so quietly the surfer had not heard or seen anything. The surfer flung himself off the board. The water was just up to his shoulders when he touched the ocean floor. He was about to start racing

The great white shark is a huge predator in the ocean.

toward shore when he saw the shark release the board. The shark sank like a submarine and disappeared back into the sea. Judging by the tooth marks on the surfboard, the shark might have been as large as 17.5 feet (5.3 m) long. The surfer was very lucky. The great white shark could have easily bitten and killed him. This shark has been considered one of the most dangerous to humans.

The great white shark has one of the largest ranges of any ocean animal. These sharks are found in all cool, **temperate**, and tropical water throughout the oceans of the world. They seem to prefer to live in areas where the water temperature is between 59 and 71 degrees Fahrenheit (15–22 °C). However, they have been found in waters ranging from 39 to 80 degrees Fahrenheit (4–27 °C). The sharks can also **migrate** thousands of miles each year to reach warmer waters.

Great white sharks live anywhere from the surface of the ocean to about 6,150 feet (1,875 m) deep. They live along the coastlines of South Africa and Australia. They

RANGE MAP

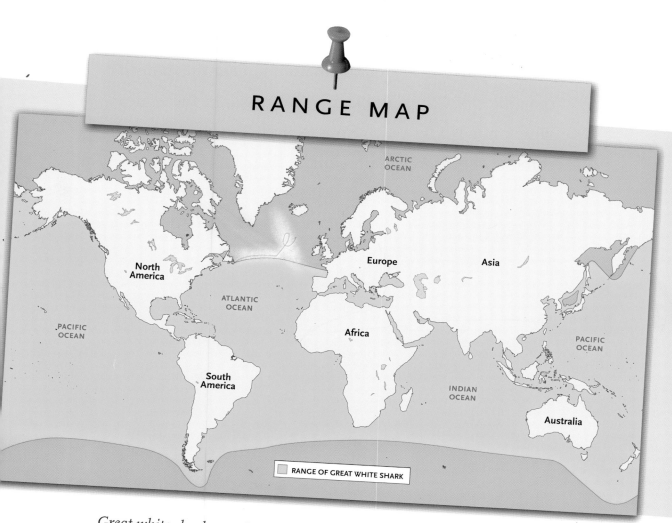

Great white sharks are found in warm and cool oceans around the world.

roam along the West, East, and Gulf Coasts of the United States. They live around Hawaii and South America. They can be found around Africa and near the eastern coastlines of China and southern Russia. In these areas, great white sharks swim close to shorelines. This is where some of their favorite prey make their homes. These are also the places humans swim and surf, which make them vulnerable to shark attacks too. ◢

Great whites can migrate to warmer
waters in cooler seasons.

LOOK AGAIN

Look at the photo closely. What can you learn
about the great white shark from this photo
that you haven't learned from the chapter?

LARGEST PREDATORY FISH

The great white shark is the world's largest known predatory fish in the ocean. Males can be about 13 feet (4 m) long. Females are larger than males and can be about 20 feet (6.1 m) long. Females can weigh around 3 tons (2.7 t). Great white sharks have torpedo-shaped bodies, powerful crescent-shaped tails, and pointed snouts.

The great white shark has excellent senses to help it hunt its prey. Its pitch-black eyes have been described as "flat" or "dead." But the great white has very good eyesight. The shark does not have eyelids to protect its eyes.

Instead, the shark can roll its eyes back into its head to help avoid injury. The great white also has an excellent sense of smell. Its sensitive nostrils can detect one drop of blood in about 25 gallons (94.6 L) of water. The shark can catch an otter's scent from 330 feet (100.6 m) away. A great white shark has good hearing as well. It can hear an otter from as far as 1.25 miles (2.0 km) away.

Great white sharks have thick bodies.

The great white also has a kind of sixth sense called **electroreception**. Located on its snout is a network of sensors called the ampullae of Lorenzini. These sensors pick up the electrical currents of an animal's muscle movements. The sensors can detect a motion as small as a heartbeat. The great white uses electroreception to locate prey from their smallest movements.

The great white has special coloring on its body. This coloring is called **countershading**. Countershading helps the shark hide from its prey when it is hunting. The great white's belly is light in color. It is usually white, light gray, or blue-gray. If prey look up at the shark, the shark's belly blends in with the light-colored water near the surface of the ocean. The shark's top half is usually a darker gray. When seen from above, this color blends in with the darker coloring of the deeper ocean. Blending in with its surroundings helps the shark sneak up on the animals it's hunting.

BODY DIAGRAM

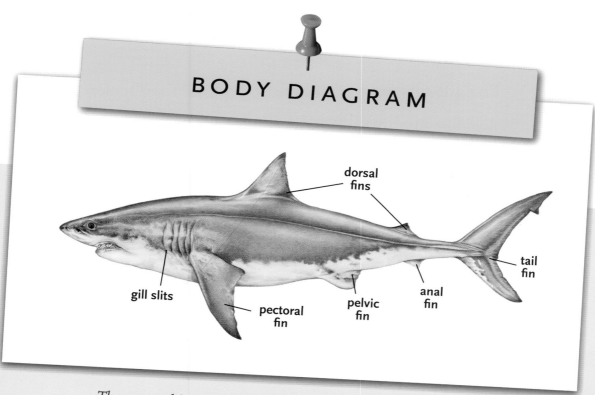

dorsal
fins

gill slits

pectoral
fin

pelvic
fin

anal
fin

tail
fin

The great white shark has a tail fin designed for fast swimming.

The great white has three main fins. It has a pectoral
fin on each side of its body. It has a large dorsal fin on
top and in the middle of its body. This triangular dorsal
fin pokes above the water if the shark swims near the
ocean surface. This sight is terrifying to many people.
The powerful tail fin pushes the shark through the
water while the other fins keep the shark balanced.

The gill slits are in front of the pectoral fins. Inside the gill slits are the gills that a shark uses to breathe. Water enters a shark's mouth and moves across the gills. The gills take oxygen out of the water. Then the water exits through the gill slits.

The great white shark has rows of **serrated**, razor-sharp teeth. It usually has about 3,000 teeth at any given time. A tooth can be about 3 inches (7.6 cm) long. A great white shark may break or lose teeth in the front. When this happens, teeth from the back rows move forward to take their place.

Great white sharks have large and incredibly sharp teeth.

The great white shark has features that help it stay afloat in the water. Its skeleton is made of **cartilage** rather than bone. A skeleton made of cartilage is about half as heavy as a bony skeleton would be. Cartilage is also more flexible than bone. This helps protect the predator. The great white also has a very large liver. The liver can weigh about 25 percent of the shark's body weight. The liver is filled with a special oil called squalene. This oil is six times lighter than salt water. Both of these traits help the heavy shark stay afloat. ◢

GO DEEPER

READ THIS CHAPTER CLOSELY. WHAT IS ITS MAIN IDEA?
PROVIDE THREE PIECES OF EVIDENCE THAT SUPPORT THIS.

MADE TO HUNT

Great white sharks are **apex** predators. This means very few animals hunt them for food. Great whites are able to eat a wide variety of foods. They will eat almost anything, including garbage or a hubcap.

However, great whites are mostly **carnivores**. They are mainly flesh-eating fish. The great white hunts and kills most of its food. But it has also been known to eat the bodies of animals that have died. Remains of sea turtles, blue sharks, and dolphins have been found in great whites' stomachs.

[21ST CENTURY SKILLS LIBRARY]

Great whites can open their mouths very wide.

LOOK AGAIN

WHAT CHARACTERISTICS CAN YOU SEE IN THIS PHOTOGRAPH THAT HELP THE SHARK HUNT AND EAT ITS PREY?

Plump seals are a favorite meal of the great white shark. Eating fat allows the great white to maintain its body temperature. It also keeps its brain warm in cold water.

The great white is also able to maintain its body temperature because it is partially **warm-blooded**. Only a few sharks are able to keep their body temperature warmer than the surrounding water. It does not matter whether the great white is hunting in cold or warm water. Its body temperature stays about the same.

It takes a great white shark a long time to digest its food. And if the shark eats something that does not agree with it, it can be slowed down for days. This can prevent the shark from catching other prey.

The great white shark has many advantages that make it a great hunter. The shark uses all its keen senses to detect food. When it finds prey, the great white can swim at up to 35 miles per hour (56.3 kmph) to chase and catch the animal. The shark can also leap out of the water to catch prey near the surface.

Great white sharks can propel themselves into the air to catch prey.

The great white uses different hunting techniques depending on the prey it's trying to catch. Elephant seals are great divers and fast swimmers. They are pretty big as well—about the size of a car. From below, the great white will see an elephant seal on the surface. The shark swims quickly, rams the seal to stun it, and then takes a bite out if it. The shark hangs back until the seal bleeds to death. Then the shark will return to feed. This allows the shark to save the energy it would have used to fight such a large animal.

Harbor seals are smaller. The great white will grab a harbor seal at the surface and pull it underwater until it drowns. Then the shark will feed near the ocean floor. The California sea lion is a faster swimmer than the harbor seal. A great white tries to attack this seal from below with a bite at its midsection. Then the shark takes the seal underwater until it stops struggling.

A great white shark sometimes "tests" its prey by taking a sample bite before it eats the whole animal.

People who have suffered shark bites are thought to be victims of such tests. Humans are not a shark's preferred meal. Humans are too skinny. A shark will test bite a human but will not eat it. ◢

Countershading helps great white sharks sneak up on prey.

CHAPTER 4

FROM PUP TO PREDATOR

Great white females do not reach maturity until they are 14 to 16 feet (4.3–4.9 m) long. Males are mature when they are 11 feet (3.4 m) long. Little is known about how great white sharks **mate**. Scientists believe it takes more than a year for the **pups** to develop. Scientists also think great white sharks give birth only every other year.

Scientists are sure about some things. The female shark carries eggs inside her body. When the eggs are fertilized, they develop in a brood chamber. The developing pups get nourishment from a yolk sac.

It is believed female great whites give birth every other year.

The pups hatch inside the female and are born soon afterward. Female great whites can have between two and ten pups in a litter. The newborns are about 5 feet (1.5 m) long. They weigh about 75 pounds (34 kg).

Scientists have not been able to observe whether great whites deliver their young in special nurseries. However, researchers believe some great whites give birth in the warmer waters along the coast of southern California. As they grow, the pups make their way to colder waters farther north and south.

Even a young shark's dorsal fin above the water could alarm a person.

LOOK AGAIN

WHAT WOULD YOU THINK IF YOU SAW A SHARK'S DORSAL FIN WHEN YOU WERE SWIMMING IN THE OCEAN? HOW WOULD YOU REACT?

As soon as the pups are born, they are able to take care of themselves. Their mother does not help them in any way. Pups know how to hunt from instinct. Young great whites have slender, pointed teeth. These are good for grasping and holding fish. The sharks eat squid and stingrays until they reach about 10 feet (3.0 m) in length at about ten years old. Then, the shape of their teeth changes. The teeth become triangular with serrated edges. This shape is better for catching larger, more solid prey such as seals and otters.

Different methods can be used to determine how long a great white shark lives. One method of determining the age involves counting the rings that form on the shark's vertebra. Researchers have found that great white sharks live to around 30 years old. ◢

Great white sharks live longer than many other shark species.

CHAPTER 5

THREATS

Because the great white shark is an apex predator, very few animals hunt it. It has few threats from nature and its natural environment. People are actually the biggest threat to the sharks. The great white shark population has decreased dramatically due to human activities. In the past 20 years, the population of great whites along the Atlantic coast of the United States has dropped 75 percent.

Great white sharks have been discovered to have high levels of toxins in their bodies. These toxins include

Fishing poses a threat to great white sharks.

pesticides and heavy metals that can harm them. Pollution caused by people is believed to be the cause of these toxins.

Great whites sometimes get caught in the nets of fishermen who are trying to catch other fish. Sharks are caught on purpose too. Sportfishermen catch the biggest sharks as trophies. These trophy sharks have usually grown to the size when reproducing is possible. When mature sharks are caught and killed, the number of pups that can be born each year goes down.

Great whites can be caught in order to sell their parts.

Great whites are also caught for their fins, jaws, and teeth. The fins are made into shark fin soup. This is a popular and expensive dish in many Asian countries. Fins can be sold for around $300 a pound. Recently, a very large set of great white shark jaws sold for $65,000. Individual shark teeth can sell for as much as $1,000.

The great white shark is labeled as Vulnerable by the International Union for Conservation of Nature (IUCN). This is the result of human actions. A Vulnerable status means the great whites aren't yet in great danger. However, if steps aren't taken to protect them, they could become endangered or **extinct**.

[21ST CENTURY SKILLS LIBRARY]

Divers studying great white sharks protect themselves by being in cages.

Great white sharks are valuable to the health of the oceans. They keep populations of ocean creatures healthy by seeking out prey that are weak or sick. Great whites eat sea animals that have died. Scientists and researchers are working to learn more about great white sharks. They hope this knowledge will help protect the sharks' presence on our planet.

THINK ABOUT IT

DISCUSS THIS CHAPTER WITH A FRIEND. WHY DO YOU THINK PEOPLE LIKE TO HUNT FOR THE GREAT WHITE SHARK? HOW WOULD YOU CONVINCE THEM TO STOP?

THINK ABOUT IT

▲ What was the most interesting fact you learned about the great white shark? Is there anything else you would like to know? Visit the library and check out another book on the great white shark. How does the information in that book compare to the information in this one?

▲ Read Chapter 3 again. Compare and contrast the different ways that a great white shark hunts for its prey. Why do you think it uses different techniques? What does this say about the great white shark?

▲ Review Chapter 4. What is the main idea in that chapter? Provide two pieces of evidence that support this point.

LEARN MORE

BOOKS

Marsico, Katie. *Sharks*. New York: Scholastic, 2011.

Musgrave, Ruth. *Everything Sharks*. Washington, DC: National Geographic, 2011.

Smith, Miranda. *Sharks*. New York: Kingfisher, 2008.

WEB SITES

National Geographic—Sharks
http://animals.nationalgeographic.com/animals/sharks

Readers discover different species of sharks, learn more about the ocean, and play games at this Web site.

Shark Trust
http://www.sharktrust.org/juniors

On this Web site, readers can watch shark videos, play games, learn fun facts, and even adopt a shark.

GLOSSARY

apex (AY-pex) at the very top

carnivore (KAR-nuh-vor) an animal that eats meat

cartilage (KAHR-tuh-lij) a hard, flexible tissue that forms certain parts of animals' bodies, such as a human ear or a shark's skeleton

countershading (KOUN-tur-shay-ding) the light and dark coloring of an animal to help it blend into its surroundings

electroreception (i-lek-tro-ri-SEP-shuhn) a type of sense that allows sharks to detect the heartbeats of their prey

extinct (ik-STINGKT) no longer found alive

mate (MATE) to join together to produce babies

migrate (MYE-grate) to move from one area to another

pup (PUP) a baby shark

serrated (SER-ay-tid) looking like the blade of a saw

temperate (TEM-pur-it) not extremely hot or cold

warm-blooded (WAHRM BLUHD-id) having a body temperature that does not change, even if the surroundings are very hot or very cold

INDEX